designer beadwork

beaded crochet designs

Ann Benson

Sterling Publishing Co. Inc., New York
A Sterling/Chapelle Book

Chapelle, Ltd., Inc.
P.O. Box 9252, Ogden, UT 84409
(801) 621-2777 • (801) 621-2788 Fax
e-mail: chapelle@chapelleltd.com
Web site: www.chapelleltd.com

Space would not permit the inclusion of every decorative item photographed for this book, nor could all of the designers be identified. Many of these items are available by contacting:

Ruby & Begonia, 204 25th Street, Ogden, UT 84401
(801) 334-7829 • (888) 888-7829 Toll-free
e-mail: ruby@rubyandbegonia.com
Web site: www.rubyandbegonia.com

Every effort has been made to ensure that all information in this book is accurate. However, due to differing conditions, tools, and individual skills, the publisher cannot be responsible for any injuries, losses, and/or other damages which may result from the use of the information in this book.

Due to limited amount of available space, we must print our patterns at a reduced size in order to give our patrons the maximum number of patterns possible in our publications. We believe the quality and quantity of our patterns will compensate for any inconvenience this may cause.

This volume is meant to stimulate craft ideas. If readers are unfamiliar or not proficient in a skill necessary to attempt a project, we urge that they refer to an instructional book specifically addressing the required technique.

Library of Congress Cataloging-in-Publication Data

Benson, Ann.
    Designer beadwork : beaded crochet designs / Ann Benson.
        p. cm.
    Includes index.
    ISBN 1-4027-2142-0
    1. Beadwork. 2. Crocheting. I. Title.

TT860.B483 2005
745.58'2--dc22

                                                        2004025675

10 9 8 7 6 5 4 3 2 1

Published by Sterling Publishing Co., Inc.
387 Park Avenue South, New York, NY 10016
©2005 by Ann Benson
Distributed in Canada by Sterling Publishing
c/o Canadian Manda Group, 165 Dufferin Street
Toronto, Ontario, Canada M6K 3H6
Distributed in Great Britain by Chrysalis Books Group PLC,
The Chrysalis Building, Bramley Road, London W10 6SP, England
Distributed in Australia by Capricorn Link (Australia) Pty. Ltd.
P. O. Box 704, Windsor, NSW 2756, Australia
Printed and Bound in China
All Rights Reserved

Sterling ISBN 1-4027-2142-0

table of contents

introduction

I like to play dress up;
It's my favorite thing;
A pocketbook, a high heel,
  a fanciful ring.
It may be a date, a party, or a prom,
  or maybe I want to pretend
  that I'm mom.
Whoever I am it's plain to see,
I like to play dress up;
And I like being me.
—Kerrie Wade

A little girl delights in trying on her mother's finery—her evening dress, her high-heeled shoes, and her best jewelry. It is a time of imagination and make-believe, when she is magically transformed into a princess and is on her way to the ball.

We have captured some of the magic here, pairing beautiful beaded crochet creations with precious little girls playing dress up out of their mommies' closets and jewelry boxes. It seems to be the perfect combination because although jewelry is both a necessity and a luxury once you are grown, when you are small, **wearing your mommy's jewelry simply makes you feel very, very pretty**.